EAGLES

CONTENTS

Introduction   4

Eagle distribution   6

Decline of the eagle

Pollution   8

Habitat destruction   10

Hunting eagles   12

Threats to survival   14

Saving the eagle

Reserves   16

Protective measures   18

Captive eagles   20

Research   22

The future   24

Eagle fact files   26-31

Index   32

© Aladdin Books Ltd 1990

*First published in
the United States in 1991 by*
Gloucester Press
387 Park Avenue South
New York NY 10016

Design Rob Hillier, Andy Wilkinson
Editor Fiona Robertson
Photo Research Cecilia Weston-Baker
Illustrations Ron Hayward Associates

Printed in Belgium

Library of Congress Cataloging-in-Publication Data

Bright, Michael.
    Eagles / Michael Bright.
      p.   cm. -- (Project wildlife)
    Includes index.
    Summary: Looks at the various species of
eagles, the many threats to their existence, and
the protective measures under way to conserve
them.
    ISBN 0-531-17262-7
    1. Eagles--Juvenile literature. 2. Birds,
Protection of--Juvenile literature. [1. Eagles. 2.
Birds--Protection.] I. Title. II. Series.
QL696.F32B73   1991
598' .916--dc20   90-43984   CIP   AC

PROJECT WILDLIFE

EAGLES

Michael Bright

Gloucester Press
New York : London : Toronto : Sydney

Introduction

The eagle is a large, powerful predator. With its head held high, it is considered by some people to be the most noble of birds. But we treat eagles less than regally. In the United States, the Bald Eagle was adopted as the nation's official emblem. Yet ironically its numbers dropped rapidly between the 1940s and 1970s, and populations have begun to recover only recently.

The problem is that eagles are apex predators, at the top of their food chain, and as such, populations are affected adversely by both natural pressures and any interference from man. Top predators are also vulnerable to problems such as egg-collecting, deliberate poisoning with baits or accidental poisoning by pesticides, and destruction of their living space. Not surprisingly, such threats have placed eagles among the world's most endangered birds.

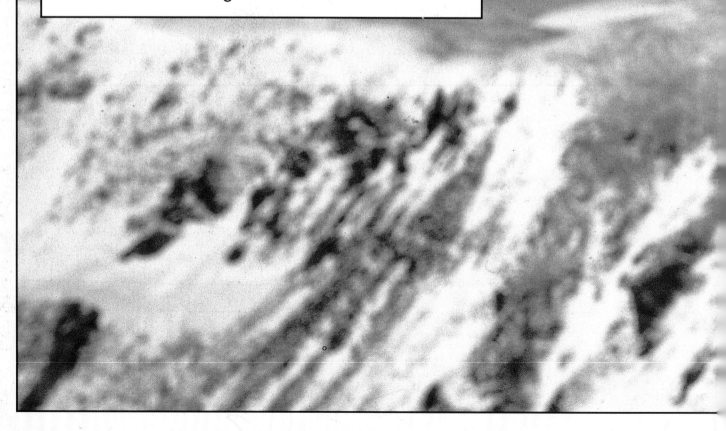

▽ The Golden Eagle is one of the most widely distributed birds of prey in the Northern Hemisphere.

Golden Eagle

White-tailed Sea Eagle

Osprey

Bald Eagle

Madagascar Sea Eagle

Harpy Eagle

Philippine Eagle

▷ The map shows the whereabouts of some of the world's rarest species of eagles. Although their distribution is widespread, the numbers of some species are very low. The White-tailed Sea Eagle, Osprey, and Bald Eagle are slowly making a comeback and are seen in places from which they had previously disappeared. The Madagascar Sea Eagle is among the world's 25 most threatened birds.

Eagle distribution

Eagles are found in almost all parts of the world although they do not necessarily stay in one locality all the year around. The Osprey is typical of many birds of prey in that it migrates. It can therefore be found, widely but thinly distributed, throughout both the Northern and Southern Hemispheres. European Ospreys spend the summer in the north and the winter in Africa, although a few birds stay close to Mediterranean shores throughout the year. North American birds migrate to Central and South America during the northern winter. The species breeds on every continent except South America. Australian Ospreys are unusual among eagles in that they are still found on Australian coasts.

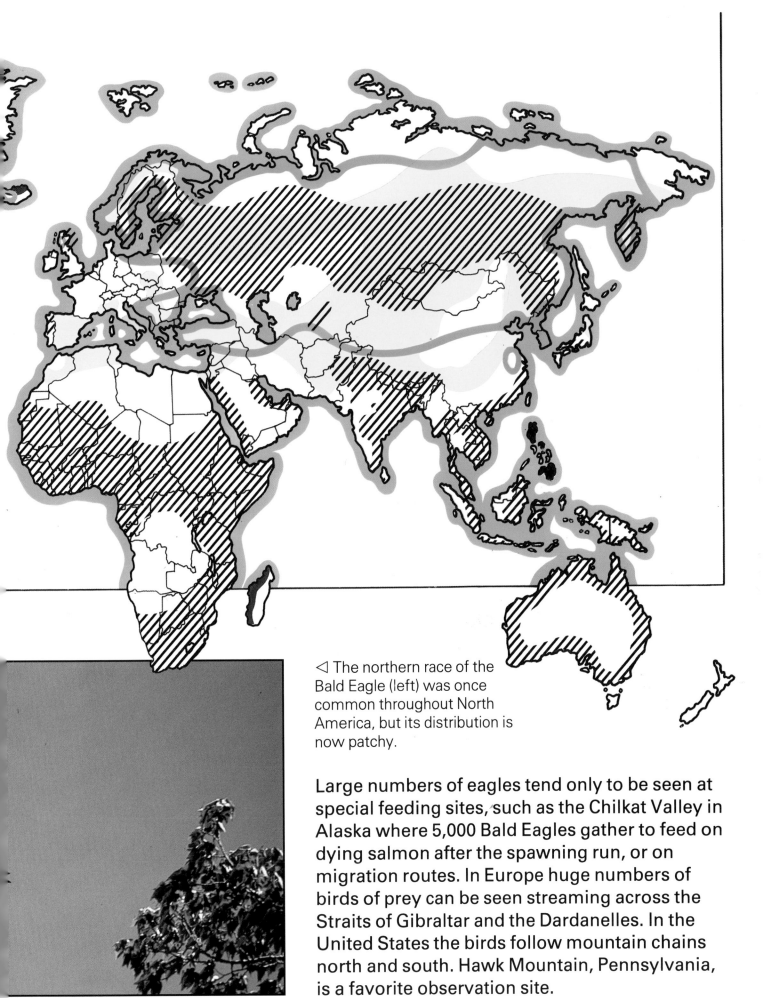

◁ The northern race of the
Bald Eagle (left) was once
common throughout North
America, but its distribution is
now patchy.

Large numbers of eagles tend only to be seen at
special feeding sites, such as the Chilkat Valley in
Alaska where 5,000 Bald Eagles gather to feed on
dying salmon after the spawning run, or on
migration routes. In Europe huge numbers of
birds of prey can be seen streaming across the
Straits of Gibraltar and the Dardanelles. In the
United States the birds follow mountain chains
north and south. Hawk Mountain, Pennsylvania,
is a favorite observation site.

Pollution

Farmers and foresters used to spray their crops with long-lasting pesticides, such as DDT, in order to kill harmful insects. Although some of the chemicals reached the target, the rest was washed away when it rained. The poison was strong enough to kill the target insects, but it should not have been lethal to birds nearby.

Nevertheless, birds were poisoned and continue to be poisoned. In New York State, the spraying of forests with DDT in the 1950s is still affecting Bald Eagles today. The problem is that pesticides like DDT are not only active for many years, but are also stored in nonlethal amounts in animal fat. However, as they pass from animal to animal in the food chain the concentrations increase at each link. Thus, top predators, such as eagles that have eaten contaminated prey, begin to store dangerous levels of the poison, which in some cases can prove fatal.

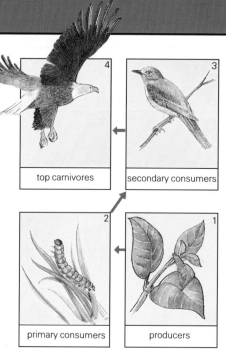

top carnivores	secondary consumers
primary consumers	producers

△ A food chain forms when a leaf is eaten by a caterpillar, which is eaten by a small bird, which in turn is eaten by a large bird.

△ DDT reaches Sea Eagles and Ospreys when it is washed from the soil into rivers, lakes and the sea. A food chain might include plankton, worms, small fish, large fish, and eagles.

◁ An eagle that hunts over land may acquire DDT from the small mammals that it kills. The mammals will have picked up the DDT on the foliage that they eat or the insects they have caught. The levels of DDT gradually accumulate within the mammal's body. High levels of stored DDT can lead to the deaths of many birds of prey.

△ Alarmed by the deaths of eagles, hawks and falcons in the 1960s, scientists began to examine not only the corpses of dead birds, but also their eggs. They made an important discovery.

They measured the thickness of the eggshells of birds of prey and found that they were much thinner than was usual. This meant that not only were adult birds at risk, but also the new generation.

When approaching the breeding season a bird puts on fat. In the fat is DDT. At egg-laying the fat is used up and DDT is released into the blood stream. This release can affect the nervous system and either kill the bird, or make it sterile. It can also cause eggshell thinning so that eggs break when incubated by the adult. By studying birds of prey, the scientists had found an important early warning system that can tell us when something is wrong in the environment.

Habitat destruction

Throughout the tropics rainforests are rapidly disappearing. The causes are many – the multimillion dollar hardwood timber industry, cattle ranching for hamburgers, and mining.

Among those affected by the disappearance of the trees are the birds of prey. The Monkey-eating Eagles of southern Asia, for example, were already threatened because of hunting and the illegal trade in live birds. Now, however, they are in decline because vast tracts of the dense dipterocarp forest in which they live are being removed. On Mindanao, one of the islands where eagles survive, the forest covered 95 percent of the island in 1910. In 1973, only 30 percent of the trees were left. Today, there are even less as 250 sq miles of forest are felled each year.

The little-known Java Hawk-eagle lives on an island the size of England, yet with double the human population. It is likely that human pressures and shrinking forest areas will mean the gradual disappearance of the species. It may become extinct before we know anything about it.

▽ The rainforests of the Amazon river basin are fast disappearing. An increase in the wealth of the ore mining industry (below) has meant a decrease in the wealth of the forest.

△ The Harpy Eagle is a casualty of deforestation in the Amazon. It needs large tracts of forest in which to hunt and catch its prey.

△ The survival of the Monkey-eating, or Philippine, Eagle may eventually depend on birds bred in captivity as its forest home disappears.

The continuing growth of the planet's human population is the main factor influencing the decline of eagle populations. People need land for homes, agriculture and industry. And as they plunder the natural world, eagles, along with other wildlife, have less space in which to hunt for food and fewer sites available for nesting.

The size of the living space and the availability of food determines how many eagles can live in a particular area. The more people, farms and factories there are, the less eagles can survive. In Spain, Imperial Eagles hunt over lowland areas and can tolerate agricultural development. Yet even some of these birds are dying.

In Scotland, the Golden Eagle is threatened not by people cutting down trees, but by new trees being planted. For the trees are the wrong kind. The new plantations consist of row after row of sterile coniferous monocultures, which do not provide the conditions necessary for Golden Eagles to catch their prey. Golden Eagles prefer large, undisturbed areas in which to hunt.

Hunting eagles

Farmers have a traditional distrust of eagles. Many eagles will scavenge on carrion as well as kill for fresh meat. A dead lamb carcass will be quickly spotted and devoured by a passing eagle. When the farmer finds it tearing at the body, however, he thinks that the eagle has killed it.

The enormous White-tailed Sea Eagle of northern Europe was a victim of this mistake because it relies more on scavenging than hunting. In Scotland in the late 18th century these eagles declined when sheep farming became widespread. Thousands of eagles were shot or poisoned by farmers protecting their livestock. By the early 20th century they had become extinct in Britain and populations were severely depleted throughout the rest of Europe. In Iceland, the poison baits were not intended for the eagles, but for Arctic foxes and owls. Yet Iceland's 80 pairs of White-tailed Sea Eagles in 1880 were reduced to seven by 1921.

Migrating eagles passing over the Lebanon on their way north in the spring and south in the autumn, are used by the local rival armies for target practice. Those that manage to survive the guns must then contend with low-flying jet fighters from the Israeli air force.

The legal shooting of eagles has often been without logic. In 1940 the birds were protected everywhere in the United States. Yet in Alaska, between 1915 and 1943, 100,000 Bald Eagles were shot to protect salmon stocks.

△ In southern Europe, eagles continue to be shot for sport. In Spain the Imperial Eagle is legally protected, yet hunters in remote areas still shoot it. It builds a large nest in a lone tree, making it an easy and conspicuous target.

Throughout its range, the Golden Eagle has been persecuted. In Scandinavia the Lapps thought the eagle killed baby reindeer until scientists found that the lynx and the wolverine were the main culprits. In North America, the sight of a single Golden Eagle sent farmers scurrying to their light aircraft from which they shot the bird out of the skies. On the grouse moors of Scotland, gamekeepers catch Golden Eagles with pole traps or kill them with poisoned baits.

▽ In Australia the sheep farmers kill Wedge-tailed Eagles. The picture below shows several birds hung on a fence to deter other eagles from coming close to livestock. However, in reality, the eagles rarely eat lambs. Instead they prefer rabbits, which are considered pests in Australia.

Threats to survival

As eagles, and their smaller relatives the hawks and falcons, become increasingly rare, their eggs become increasingly more valuable. And, when there are valuable objects like birds' eggs to be collected, then there is always somebody who will collect them, even if the practice is illegal.

Eagles are also sought by illegal traders, who take eggs or young birds for breeding. In 1982, a survey revealed that in Britain thefts of wild birds of prey had doubled within that year. Golden Eagles are sold for two thousand dollars each. The illegal traders try to avoid detection by collecting eggs from the wild and rearing the birds in captivity. They are then given false papers which show that the birds are captive-bred and may be sold legally. In the long, dry summer of 1976 in Britain, at least 36 Peregrine nests, or aeries, were known to have been raided by egg collectors.

In Zimbabwe in 1984 a leading ornithologist and his son were convicted of stealing and smuggling birds' eggs. When the police visited his house they found 900 blown Black Eagles' eggs, each worth $1,800. They had removed the eggs from nests and falsified the data they recorded. They even pretended to have observed nesting, feeding of young, and fledging at the nest from which they had stolen the eggs. They were fined $5,000 and given four suspended prison sentences.

△ The rare Gyrfalcon (above) of Scandinavia is a favorite among falconers and can command prices of over $80,000 on the market.

△ Numbers of Peregrine Falcons are slowly recovering across the northern hemisphere after suffering from the effects of DDT.

△ The false information recorded by the Zimbabwe ornithologist about the Black Eagle means the status of the bird is unsure.

That the trade in live birds of prey and their eggs is big international business was revealed in 1985 by Operation Falcon. Investigators from the US Fish and Wildlife Service uncovered an international black market which involved egg collectors, smugglers and traders from America, Britain, Finland, West Germany, France, Australia, Iceland, Canada and Saudi Arabia.

Birds were taken from North America and sold illegally in Europe and the Middle East. Thirty nine people were arrested in the United States, 13 in Canada. The illegal Canadian trade alone netted $750,000 in two years. During the first three years of Operation Falcon, officials monitored the illegal trading of 400-500 birds. They estimated that this represented only 10 percent of the actual trade. The main target was the Gyrfalcon. Only 4,000-5,000 North American birds are thought to remain in the wild.

▽ The nests of birds of prey tend to be inaccessible – on clifftops, on mountains, or in the tops of trees. Nest robbers must risk life and limb to steal the eggs. Then they must avoid detection during transit. During Operation Falcon officials discovered eggs that were hidden in stockings and stuffed inside the courier's shirt, and others secreted in a cosmetics vanity case carried by a smuggler's girlfriend. On their way to the Middle East, eggs and young birds, supplied with false documentation, often travel first class.

Reserves

All over the world people began to realize that many species of birds of prey were being threatened by shooting, poisoning by pesticides, and habitat destruction, and that measures had to be taken to save them. Many eagles are migrants and so it is difficult to protect them.

Nevertheless, at Hawk Mountain in the Appalachian Mountains a 2,000 acre refuge was created as far back as 1934 to protect migrant birds of prey. In days gone by, poachers would hide among the rocks. From there they ambushed birds as they followed the mountains on their way north and south. Today, 40,000 visitors a year lie in wait for the migrants, represented by 14 species of eagles, hawks and falcons. They are greeted not with guns, but with binoculars and cameras.

At their destination, birds of prey can be more easily protected. They can be provided with a safe haven in which to build their nests and rear their young. One of the first actions taken by bird conservationists, therefore, was to create wildlife reserves and refuges in which birds of prey could breed undisturbed.

△ At Scotland's Loch Garten (above) one of the last remaining remnants of the ancient Caledonian forest is being preserved. Careful management of the reserve has meant that visitors can now witness the return of the Osprey, without disturbing the birds. Ospreys are also fairly common in America. They live mainly along the coast, such as on Long Island and along the Hudson River.

"They don't blink at shelling. It looks to me like we've done them a left-handed favor by just keeping this much land open and secluded."

Joe Ondek, environment specialist at the Aberdeen Gunnery Range, Maryland, home of one of the largest concentrations of Bald Eagles outside Alaska.

In Spain the last stronghold of the endangered Iberian race of the Imperial Eagle has been the Coto Donana National Park, in Andalucia. Throughout the rest of Spain the eagle is still shot by farmers, but in the reserve it is relatively safe. Since 1972 the third and fourth chicks have been removed from the nest, bred in captivity, and rereleased into the wild. Not only do these chicks grow into strong adult birds, they have also helped stock new reserves in Caceres province.

△ The Imperial Eagle of Spain and Portugal is identified by the white leading edge to the wing. There are about 104 breeding pairs in Spain and a few in Portugal, with 13 pairs in the Coto Donana National Park. The captive breeding of the third and fourth chicks has meant a 43 percent increase in the number of fledglings.

Protective measures

The White-tailed Sea Eagle is Europe's largest eagle. It was also one of the rarest. Twice its numbers have declined drastically, particularly in Scandinavia and Britain. First it was persecuted by sheep farmers because it fed on dead sheep and was accused of killing them, and second it suffered from the effects of DDT and eggshell thinning. The Finnish population was reduced to 20 pairs, the Swedish to four pairs and the bird disappeared altogether from Scotland and Denmark. Its last stronghold was in Norway, where half of Europe's population still remains.

Then in 1971, a recovery program was started in Sweden. Breeding sites, previously disturbed by timber cutting and building projects, were protected in nature reserves. Winter feeding with pesticide-free meat reduced the intake of DDT and ensured the survival of young birds during their first winter.

▽ The captive rearing of eagle chicks, like those in the picture (below left), and their reintroduction into the wild has had some success. Populations of Bald Eagles in North America, Imperial Eagles in Spain, and Monkey-eating Eagles in southern Asia have all benefited from this technique.

Sometimes the best laid plans can backfire. In the Philippines a lot of American and British conservation money was put into rearing Monkey-eating Eagles. However, guerillas robbed the breeding stations, and the government sold half of the forest into which the birds were to be introduced to land speculators.

In Scotland the White-tailed Sea Eagle story was even more dramatic. In 1959 and 1968 birds were brought from Norway to Fair Isle, but the birds failed to survive to breeding age.

However, in 1975 a new reintroduction program was started. 72 birds were flown by the Royal Air Force from Bodo in Norway to Kinloss in Scotland, and then by road and boat to the Isle of Rhum on Scotland's west coast.

Special food dumps helped the birds through the winter. Half of them survived and, following unsuccessful attempts to breed in 1983 and 1984, in 1985 four pairs mated and reared their young. The first native-born White-tailed Sea Eagles for 70 years flew once more over Scotland.

◁ The Bald Eagle (left) has been reared successfully in unique experiments that combine natural and artificial methods of rearing. Chicks are hatched in the laboratory and then introduced, when a few weeks old, into the nest of a wild foster parent.

Captive eagles

Populations of Bald Eagles in many parts of North America are showing signs of recovery. Control of the use of DDT since Dec 31, 1972, has contributed to the success. But, the loss of habitat is still worrying scientists. The Wyoming Game and Fish Department has estimated that a large eagle population in the Jackson Hole area could be gone within 10 years if something is not done to protect the birds' habitat.

Captive breeding programs have therefore been introduced in an attempt to return eagles to the areas from which they have disappeared altogether. The chicks are first reared at places like the Patuxent Wildlife Research Center in Maryland and then distributed around the country where they are placed in the nests of foster parents. Five eagle recovery teams in the United States monitor their progress.

The very rare Monkey-eating Eagle is protected by law and its capture is strictly regulated. The Philippines Parks and Wildlife Service has been allowed to take 18 birds into captivity for breeding, but so far success has been limited. There are only about 300 of these eagles left in the wild.

▷ The Bald Eagle chicks are either taken from captive birds (right), or from the nests of birds in the wild. They are hand reared until about 15 days old. Then the small, downy chick is taken to the nest of the surrogate parents. This often involves a forestry official climbing 89 ft into a tall pine tree and placing the chick in the platform of twigs the eagles have constructed.

◁ This Monkey-eating Eagle, seen with its surrogate human "mother," has been reared in captivity in order to start a new breeding colony. After the success of the Bald Eagle captive breeding experiments, the guardians of other eagle populations are trying the same techniques. It may be the only way that some of the rarer species of eagles will survive.

Many eagles and their relatives are reared in zoos and sanctuaries, where they spend their entire lives. Some conservationists feel these collections are important for introducing people to birds of prey. It is an opportunity to explain that traditional notions about eagles and young livestock, for example, may be wrong and that eagles should be seen as making a much more positive contribution even in a farming environment. Eagles clear dead carcasses and reduce the risk of disease, and they may help to control agricultural pests such as rabbits.

"We're running an eagle factory here. Our goal is to place eagles back in the wild areas where they once flourished."

Steve Sherrod, Director of the Sutton Avian Research Center, near Bartlesville, Oklahoma.

Research

Eagle researchers in temperate latitudes must be patient, have a head for heights, and be prepared to stay out in all weathers. Many research techniques are used, ranging from observation with telescopes and binoculars, to ringing and remote tracking with radio transmitters and satellites. Information must be gathered over many years before a detailed picture of eagle life can be obtained.

In many parts of the world this historical perspective is missing because people have only just realized that their eagles are in trouble. But, in the Appalachian Mountains, one visionary bought the land around Hawk Mountain and put a young naturalist in charge. He not only evicted the poachers, but also recorded all events that took place. Today we have over thirty years of information about bird sightings, and migration patterns which enables scientists to predict the passage of birds of prey.

△ In order to keep a close watch on eagles in and around their inaccessible nests, scientists construct comfortable hides and watchtowers (above).

▽ Amateur birdwatchers like those in the picture below may contribute a great deal to our understanding of eagle life and behavior.

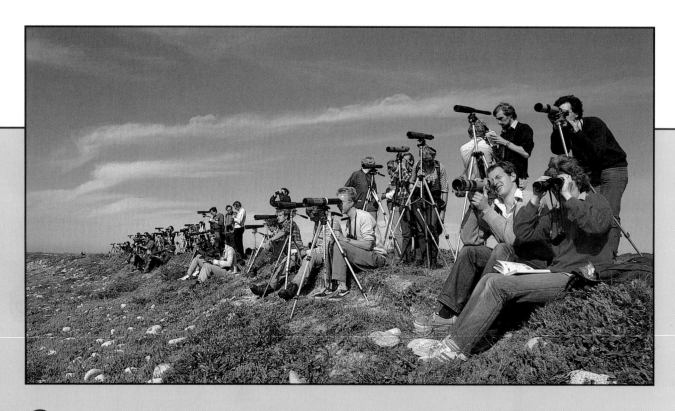

Many observations of an eagle's daily life can be seen from afar. But in order to monitor closely the development of eagle chicks and behavior at the nest, researchers must place themselves in some very dangerous places indeed. To reach the nests, they may have to climb tall trees, scale mountains or sea cliffs, or be lowered down to narrow ledges below rocky crags. In some places, daily observations are made from very tall but rickety places that overlook a nest.

However, scientists have to be careful that they do not disturb the birds unnecessarily, frightening away parents and bringing breeding for that year to a halt. There is considerable controversy, for example, about the way researchers interfered with the few remaining California Condors in western America. Some scientists believe that the constant observations and capture programs hastened the bird's decline in the wild.

In the United States, Bald Eagles have been fitted with lightweight transmitters and their progress monitored from satellites in space. One individual visited eight Atlantic coast states in the winter months and returned without fail to the area where it was hatched to breed during the summer.

▽ The young Golden Eagle in the nest is being tagged with a colored and numbered ring around its leg. This will identify the bird for the rest of its life. Scientists can then monitor its progress. By following the fortunes of many individuals, scientists can build up a detailed picture of an eagle's daily life.

The future

The future for some species of eagles is unclear. After the ravages of shooting and the disastrous effects of DDT, the destruction of living space is pushing many species toward extinction. Species such as the North American Bald Eagle and European White-tailed Sea Eagle, are recovering. But they are not safe yet, as another, more serious problem begins to emerge. In the 1960s the Peregrine Falcon succumbed to the problems of DDT and populations across the Northern Hemisphere dwindled. A ban on DDT in the 1970s and careful conservation efforts since then have enabled populations to recover.

But recently coastal-based Peregrines have been showing all the symptoms that their land-based relatives had shown thirty years ago. Yet nobody has been using DDT. It seems that the DDT spread on the land in the 1950s and 1960s has been washed via the rivers into the sea and it is only now, more than three decades later, appearing in the marine food chain. DDT was intended as a short-term solution to a farming problem, but instead has become a long-term nightmare for the environment.

The Serpent Eagle is one of the six rarest birds in the world. Some people believe there may be a few survivors in India and Central Europe. Their future depends on preserving the remaining rainforest, but it is expected that all lowland forests will be removed over the next few years.

▽ An eagle chick begins its perilous life, but will it have a place in which to live?

The Bald Eagle is, perhaps, a symbol of hope for all birds of prey. Its recovery from the brink of extinction shows that, if the will is there, something can be done to save our endangered eagles. Across the North American continent the majestic Bald Eagle is once more the monarch of the skies.

Eagle fact file 1

The eagles with the greatest recorded wingspan were a female Wedge-tailed Eagle in Tasmania and a female Golden Eagle from Yorkshire, both with 9 ft wingspan. The largest eagle is the Harpy Eagle of South America with an average weight of 17 lb. The heaviest known eagle was a gigantic Harpy from Guyana that weighed in at 27 lb.

Types of eagle

Eagles can be divided up into several groups. The fish-catching Osprey is in a family all of its own. The eleven species of strikingly colored fish-eating eagles include the American Bald Eagle, the African Fish Eagle, the black-and-white Steller's Sea Eagle of Japan and the White-tailed Sea Eagle (below left) of northern Europe and Asia. The twelve snake eagles include the very rare Madagascar Serpent Eagle, and the red-faced Bateleur of Africa.

The 53 species of buzzards and harpies include the Common Buzzard and Rough-legged Buzzard of Europe and Asia, the rare Philippine Monkey-eating Eagle (below right) from southern Asia, and the Harpy Eagle of South America. The 30 species of true, or booted, eagles include the enormous Golden Eagles of the Northern Hemisphere, the two races of Imperial Eagles, the African Hawk Eagle and the Martial and Crowned Eagles, and the Australian Wedge-tailed Eagle.

Characteristics

Most eagles are large and powerful predatory birds. They have bodies adapted for a search-and-kill method of hunting. The large wings mean they can soar with little effort and search over a wide area. They have keen eyesight for spotting a target at a distance, powerful legs and feet for grasping prey, and large, heavy hooked beaks for tearing meat. The Osprey is camouflaged with brown plumage above and white below. Sea eagles are recognized by the white plumage around the head and neck. The curious Palm-nut Vulture, which eats the nuts of oil palms, retains its powerful talons and can turn to predation when palms are scarce.

The Indian Black Eagle is also unusual in having long toes and thin talons for plucking a nest full of chicks from a tree. Forest eagles like the Crowned Eagle and the Harpy Eagle have short wings and a long tail for maneuverability. The Bateleur has long, pointed wings and a short tail. It glides at speed with a wobbly flight that compensates for the small tail. European Snake Eagles, which hunt in open country, have a large tail that can be fanned out to give more lift when hovering. The larger eagles that soar effortlessly in mountainous country have long, broad wings. The primary feathers at the end of the wings are constantly adjusted to keep the head and body steady.

The Imperial Eagle (above) of Spain and Portugal has the characteristic head, beak, talons and wings of a mountain eagle, but it is much slower and less maneuverable. It hunts over lowland areas by spotting from a vantage point or soaring overhead.

The strongest eagle for its size is thought to be Pallas's Fish Eagle which can carry twice its own weight. Steller's Sea Eagle, which eats seals as well as fish, can carry more than its own weight. In Norway a White-tailed Sea Eagle once carried off a baby girl.

Eagle fact file 2

Feeding

Eagles eat a variety of foods including mammals, birds, reptiles and amphibians, fish, insects, and even nuts. Steppe Eagles in Africa have been known to catch anything from a termite to a mole rat. Some eagles perform amazing aerobatics to catch a meal: the Harpy Eagle can fly rapidly through the forest canopy, turn upside down, pluck a large sloth from the underside of a branch and fly to a bough where it tears into its meal. The Osprey sometimes appears to be drowning when it plunges feet-first into the water and, with great difficulty carries away an enormous trout or salmon.

Most eagles catch their prey with their feet and despatch the victim with the beak. The attack is swift. Small mammals are often surprised in the open, although Golden Eagles sometimes fly in low behind hills or bushes and catch an alert animal, like a hare, before it can escape. Birds are snatched and killed in flight. Some eagles, such as the Bateleur and Tawny Eagle, behave like pirates and harass other birds in order to get them to drop their catch. Parents occasionally rob their youngsters or their mate. And if they cannot catch anything live, many eagles will turn to carrion. Anything from beached whales to dead lambs will suffice.

The African Fish Eagle does not usually plunge into the water like an osprey, but plucks a fish from just below the surface with its powerful talons.

Talons

Eagles use their talons to seize but not to kill the prey. The Harpy Eagle (below) has large talons with which it can grab its prey.

The feet of the African Fish Eagle (below) have rough spicules on the bottom of the toes to help it grasp the struggling prey, often a slippery wet fish.

The Crowned Eagle has thick-toed, powerful feet (below) with which it can exert a paralyzing grip on prey as large as antelope, such as adult forest duikers.

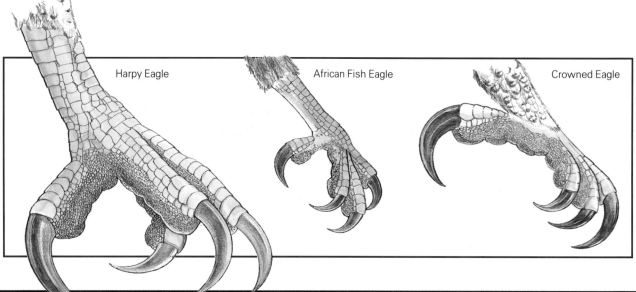

Harpy Eagle   African Fish Eagle   Crowned Eagle

Migration

Some eagles, particularly those breeding in temperate regions like the Golden Eagle (above) and Osprey, migrate along well-known routes. Birds in Alaska and Siberia fly south to escape the harsh winter, whereas birds in California and Scotland may simply migrate to the lower slopes of mountains. Other eagles are nomadic. Those, such as the Wedge-tailed Eagle, move from place to place in response to changes in the weather and food availability. Bateleurs are grounded when wet and so avoid places with heavy rain.

Eagles mainly migrate overland, particularly along mountain chains or along the tops of escarpments and rift valley walls. They ride on the thermals of rising hot air warmed by the sun. They spiral up in one thermal to great heights and then glide long distances to the next thermal. Thunderclouds are sometimes favored because they produce strong updrafts. But bad weather can bring migration to a halt. A bird cannot soar with wet feathers. A Steppe Eagle was once found dead high on Mt. Everest, the victim of bad weather.

When conditions are favorable for soaring and gliding, an eagle might travel 400-500 miles in a day. It can reach speeds of up to 50mph. Steppe Eagles migrate the furthest of all the eagles. Each spring, some may fly from their over-wintering sites in southern Africa, via Suez, to breeding sites in central Eurasia. In the autumn they take the same route back, taking six to eight weeks to complete the journey. Most eagles do not eat when migrating, although the prospect of food in a locust swarm can sidetrack a hungry migrant.

Eagle fact file 3

The breeding cycle of eagles can vary considerably. In Kenya, the time between nest-building and independence of the young can be five months for African Fish Eagles, and 22 months for Crowned Eagles. Crowned Eagle fledglings depend on their parents for up to 11 months.

Courtship

Eagles have several nuptial displays. A pair of Martial Eagles may perch and call alone or together to start their courtship. Male and female Crowned Eagles have a vigorous nuptial flight. The male climbs to 1,000 ft, plunges with wings folded for 200 ft, swings up again almost to his former height, flaps his wings at the top, and then dives again.

The male and female of some species roll in flight and touch feet. The African Fish Eagle is more dramatic. The pair starts courtship by soaring and calling. At the climax of the display, they put on a remarkable aerobatic performance. The two birds soar to a great height, grasp talons and whirl, either in a series of tumbling cartwheels or in a more gentle lateral spin, and fall out of the sky.

Eagles display at other times besides during courtship. In the threat display, a bird literally "spread-eagles," with its wings open, the head feathers raised and the mouth open. It is used to deter potential predators approaching the nest.

The young Bald Eagles in the picture above are fighting with their most dangerous weapons – their talons. When times are hard and food is scarce, territorial fights often break out over the right to eat a particular morsel of food.

Bateleurs are merciless with intruders. First they perform a distraction and threat display. They jump up and down, flapping half-opened wings, and call loudly. If the intruder does not go they attack with flapping wings and chase it away.

Nests

Many species of eagles build a large and solid platform nest, or aerie, of tangled twigs and branches. It is used for many years, with a new piece being added each breeding season. The largest known nests have been made by Bald Eagles. A nest in Ohio was 13 ft deep and 8½ ft across, and was the result of 36 years work. Another in Florida was 20 ft deep and 10 ft across.

The young

Incubation of the eggs lasts about forty days, after which the eagle chick takes several days to emerge from the shell. A newly hatched Golden Eagle weighs about 4 oz. It is fed a number of small meals at first, taking more food after a couple of days. The first chick to hatch is usually a few days ahead of its brother or sister. When the second hatches the siblings fight wildly and the firstborn dominates the other, taking most of the food. The second, third or fourth to hatch often die. The parents ignore the fighting and continue to feed the survivor. It fledges in 65-70 days. The young eagle will return to the nest for periods varying between a few days for Snake Eagles, to almost a year in the larger eagles.

Index

A aeries 14
African Fish Eagle 30
apex predators 4, 8
Australian Ospreys 6

B Bald Eagle 4, 6, 7, 8, 18,
19, 20, 23, 24, 25
Bateleur 27
bird-watchers 22
Black Eagle 14, 27
breeding 6, 9, 11, 15, 20,
23, 30, 31
breeding sites 18
buzzards 26

C California Condors 23
captive-bred birds 14,
17, 18, 19, 20
captive eagles 20, 21
Chilkat Valley 7
Coto Donana National
Park 17
courtship 30
Crowned Eagle 27

D DDT 8, 9, 14, 18, 20, 24
deforestation 10, 11, 18,
24
display 30
distribution 6, 7

E egg-collecting 4, 14, 15
eggs 9, 18
extinction 10, 12, 23, 24

F falconers 14, 15, 21
fat 9

feeding 28, 30
feeding sites 7
food chain 4, 8, 9, 24
future 24

G Golden Eagle 5, 11, 13,
14, 23, 26
Gyrfalcon 14, 15

H habitat destruction 4, 10,
11, 16, 20
harpies 26
Harpy Eagle 11, 26, 27
Hawk Mountain 7, 16, 22
hunting 10, 12, 13, 16,
22, 24

I illegal trade 14, 15
Imperial Eagle 11, 12,
17, 18, 27

J Java Hawk-eagle 10

L legal hunting 12
Loch Garten 16

M Madagascar Sea Eagle 6
Madagascar Serpent
Eagle 24
Martial Eagle 30
migration 6, 12, 16, 29
Monkey-eating Eagle 10,
18, 19, 20

N nesting 11
nests 15, 22, 23, 31

O Operation Falcon 15
Osprey 6, 9, 16, 26, 27

P Pallas's Fish Eagle 27
Palm-nut Vulture 27
Peregrine Falcon 14, 24
pesticides 4, 8, 9, 16, 18
poison 4, 8, 9, 12, 13, 16
pollution 4, 8, 9
population 4, 6, 7
preservation 12, 16,
18-21, 24

R rainforest 10, 11, 24
reintroduction 18, 19
research 22, 23
reserves 16-18

S satellite monitoring 23
scavenging 12, 18, 21
Sea Eagles 9, 27
Snake Eagles 27
sport 12-14
Steppe Eagle 29

T tagging 23
talons 28
Tawny Eagle 28

U United States 4

W Wedge-tailed Eagle 13,
26
White-tailed Sea Eagle 6,
12, 18, 19, 24, 27

Z zoos 21

Photographic Credits

Cover and pages 19, 21 and 26 right: Survival Anglia; pages 4-5 and 14 middle: Planet Earth Pictures; pages 6-7 and 25: J. Allan Cash Library; pages 8, 9 right, 10, 11 left, 12, 13, 14 left and right, 15, 17, 18, 24, 26 left and 29: Bruce Coleman Ltd; pages 9 left, 11 right, 16, 22 bottom, 23 and 31 bottom: Frank Lane Agency; pages 20, 22 top and 30: Ardea; page 27: Roger Vlitos; page 31 top: David Hoskings.

PRINTED IN BELGIUM BY

proost
INTERNATIONAL BOOK PRODUCTION